Questions AND Answers

KNIGHTS AND CASTLES

Philip Brooks

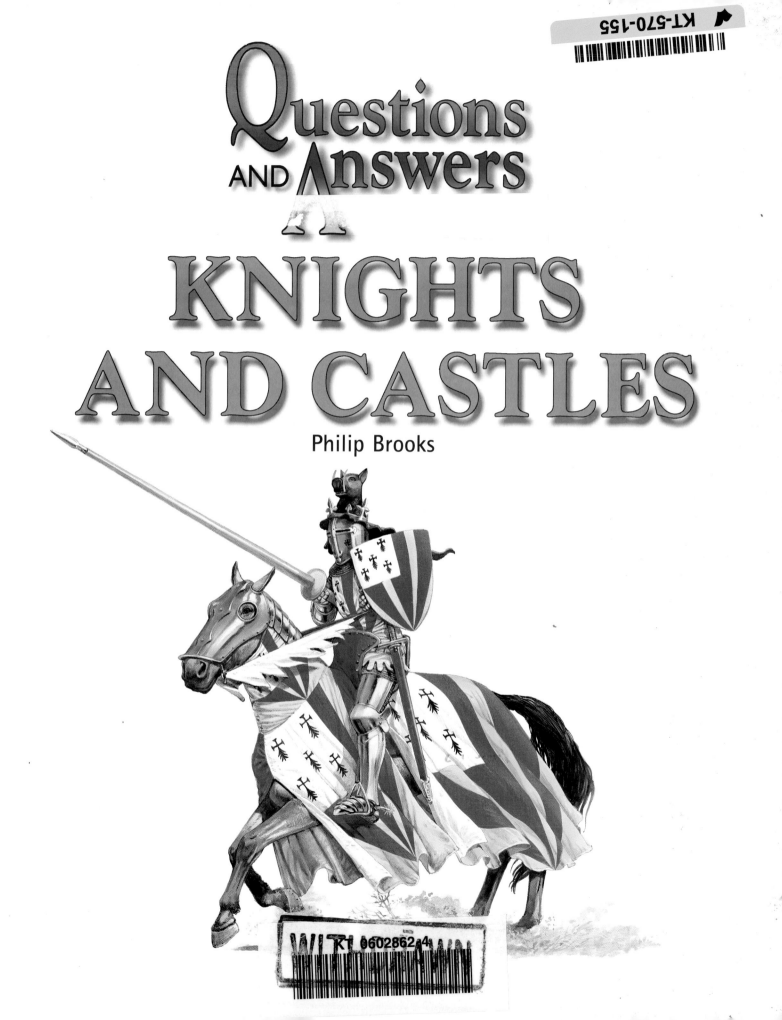

KINGFISHER
Kingfisher Publications Plc
New Penderel House
283-288 High Holborn
London WC1V 7HZ
www.kingfisherpub.com

Produced by Scintilla Editorial Ltd
33 Great Portland Street
London W1W 8QG

First published by Kingfisher Publications Plc in 2001
10 9 8 7 6 5 4 3 2 1

1TR/0301/TIM/UNV/MA130

ISBN 0 7534 0547 4

Printed in China

Author: Philip Brooks
Editor: Fergus Collins
Art editor: Keith Davis
Designer: Joe Conneally

Illustrations: Francis D'Ohani, Kevin Toy, J. Gower,
G D Achille/Artist Partners, Martin Hargreaves, Nikki Palin,
Adam Hook, Angus McBride, Eddy Krähenbühl, Julian Baker,
Peter Dennis/Linda Rogers Agency, Ray Grinaway,
Lee Edwards, David McAllister/Simon Girling,
Shirley Tourret, Steiner Lund, Christa Hook/Linden Artists,
Nick Harris/Virgil Pomfret, John James

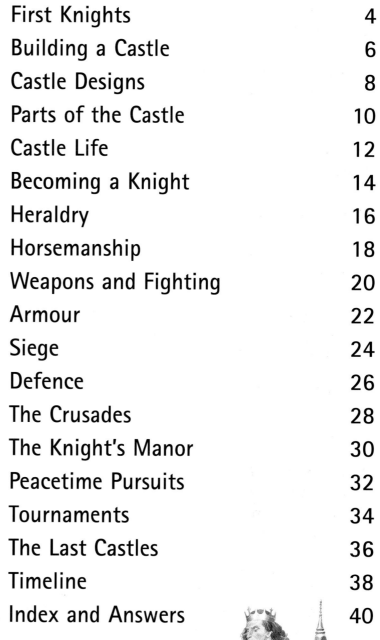

Contents

First Knights

Knights were noblemen who fought on horseback and often lived in castles. This lifestyle began in the early Middle Ages (see page 38) in France, and spread across Europe. Knights were successful because they were part of a system that helped kings win wars and govern their kingdoms. It was known as the feudal system.

The king

Roman cavalryman

Goth horseman

Who were the first knights?

Knights and feudalism arrived when Charlemagne (right) created his empire in the ninth century. Earlier, the Romans had used mounted soldiers, but their role in battle was limited. Some of the European peoples ruled by the Romans, such as the Celts and Goths, were good horsemen and fought on horseback. But they had no feudal system and so were not true knights.

How did the feudal system work?

In a country with the feudal system, the king owned all the land, but he distributed some of the land to his lords – who were knights. This 'gift' provided a knight with an income, but in return he had to fight for the king and help run the kingdom. In turn, the knight allowed peasants to make a living from his land as long as they also worked for him.

Who was Charlemagne?

Charlemagne was the king of the Franks, a people who occupied France and western Germany. From his base at Aachen, he built up a huge empire. He set up local lords as governors of each area, giving them land in return for service – creating an early feudal system. In the year 800, he was given the title of Roman emperor, although the true Roman empire had fallen 300 years earlier.

Why were the Normans so powerful?

The Normans (left) were people who originally came from Scandinavia and settled in northwestern France. They were good builders and erected many strong castles. Like their Viking ancestors, they were skilled soldiers, sailors and boat-builders. Unlike the Vikings, they also had a feudal system. All these factors helped them to create a kingdom in France and England and to rule it effectively. The Normans also carved out dominions in southern Italy and the Middle East.

What were mottes and baileys?

Mottes and baileys were the first true castles. When the Normans conquered England they needed castles quickly as bases for their lords. They made an earth mound, called a motte, and built a wooden tower on top as a stronghold. Next to this they fenced off a yard, called a bailey, where they built a hall, stables, a chapel and other buildings. A ditch or moat surrounded the castle.

Motte

Bailey

How could you tell a high-ranking Norman?

A high-ranking Norman (above) rode a horse, carried a kite-shaped shield and wore mail armour. He wielded a sword and lance, and on his lance he tied a small flag, called a pennon, which showed he was a noble.

Were wooden castles weak?

Wooden castles were well protected by their earth mounds and moats, but they were easy to knock down or to attack with fire. Most of them were eventually replaced by stronger stone buildings.

Building a Castle

Skilled craftsmen were needed to build a castle, including masons to work stone, carpenters to build floors and roofs and metalworkers to make bars and fastenings for doors. The master mason, who designed the castle, supervised all these activities, and made sure the building was extremely strong.

How quickly could you build a castle?

The Normans could put up a wooden castle in a few days, but a big stone castle (right) could take years to construct. Castle builders had no modern tools. They had to rely on simple aids like treadmills for lifting heavy loads, together with wooden scaffolding and ladders to reach to the tops of high walls.

How did stone masons cut large blocks of stone?

Stone masons (above) used large, two-man saws to cut stone roughly. They then marked the stone with dividers and set-squares before shaping it more precisely with chisels. They did as much work as they could at the quarry in order to save time and energy. By removing all the unwanted stone, the masons did not have to cart too much extra weight to the building site.

Why do the stairs wind up to the right?

With the stairs going this way, a right-handed defender could easily use his weapon. The attacker coming up the stairs found it harder to swing his sword.

How did they build the walls?

Castle builders liked to use neat, rectangular stone blocks for the walls – if they could get them – shaped with a mallet and chisel. These would be bonded together tightly with cement (right) so that an attacker would find it difficult to break them down. Laid carefully, these blocks could even be used for the curves needed for round castle towers. For extra strength, rubble and cement were packed into the main walls (see page 9).

(see page 9)

How did workers lift large stones into position?

Carrying heavy lumps of stone up to the castle battlements was hard work. Masons used a rope and pulley, which they linked to a simple wooden winch (left), to haul up the stone. At the end of the rope they could attach either a basket for small stones, or a pair of pincer-like metal grabbers, for a larger block.

Why did they turn timber?

Carpenters used a tool called a lathe to make rounded items like posts. Powered by a long, springy pole (right), the lathe could spin a piece of wood at speed. The carpenter held his chisel on the wood, removing the corners and giving it a round shape. This process was called turning.

How were planks cut from massive tree trunks?

Medieval carpenters used a pit and a long, two-handled saw (above) to cut right along the length of a tree trunk. One man stood inside the pit, pulling the saw downwards, while the other held the top end of the saw, guiding it carefully along. Once they had begun to saw away, the workers drove wooden wedges into the gap to keep the cut open. One large trunk could make several planks.

Quick-fire Quiz

1. What gave the lathe its power?
a) A springy pole
b) A water wheel
c) A motor

2. What was scaffolding made from?
a) Stone
b) Metal poles
c) Wooden poles

3. What did masons use to grip large stone blocks?
a) Hands
b) Metal grabbers
c) Baskets

4. How many men usually worked at a saw pit?
a) One
b) Two
c) Three

Castle Designs

Castle builders tried all sorts of different designs to make their buildings stronger. One of the simplest was the square stone tower, or keep. But a keep was not enough on its own and was usually surrounded by extra walls. Later, builders added towers, gatehouses and more walls.

Why were some towers round?

Round towers were stronger than square towers, because they did not have weak corners. In addition, defenders could fire arrows in many different directions from a round tower, giving them more chance of hitting their enemies. Not all towers were round, but their importance for defence made them increasingly popular.

What was a shell keep?

A shell keep was a circular stone wall on top of an earth mound. Many of these were built on the site of old motte and bailey castles. Around the inside of a shell keep was a wall walk, where defenders could stand to shoot through the battlements. Below this were structures such as the hall set against the outer wall.

Why have extra sets of walls?

Early castles had just one set of walls. This made it fairly easy for an attacker to break inside, so builders began adding extra sets of walls (right). This slowed attackers down. It also meant that defenders could trap their enemies between two walls, making them sitting targets for defending archers.

Where was the castle strongest?

In early castles, the stronghold was usually the keep. But when keeps went out of fashion, the gatehouse (above) became the strongest part. Gatehouses had thick walls, twin towers, and one or more strong gates, called portcullises (see page 27). Outside the main walls, lords sometimes built a barbican, a strong outer courtyard that an enemy would have to take before attacking the main castle.

Outer bailey

Ditch

Wooden hoardings

How thick were the walls?

Stone castle walls could be several metres thick. The thicker they were, the harder they were for attackers to knock down. If they were really thick, enemies might not even bother to attack them. Sometimes, a castle wall was actually made up of two parallel walls. The gap between them could be filled with rubble for extra strength.

What was a concentric castle?

A concentric castle was a castle with two parallel sets of walls, one inside the other. As well as giving an enemy two barriers to get through, these twin walls provided defenders with two firing platforms. The outer wall was often lower than the one on the inside, so that one group of defending archers could fire safely over the heads of the others.

Chateau Gaillard (begun 1196)

Battlements

Keep

Inner wall

Inner bailey

Round tower

Outer wall

Quick-fire Quiz

1. Where did archers stand in a shell keep?
a) In the courtyard
b) On the wall walk
c) On the catwalk

2. Why did archers like round towers?
a) They gave more lines of fire
b) They were warm
c) They were spacious

3. What was a portcullis?
a) A type of tower
b) A strong gate
c) A thick wall

4. What were extra walls for?
a) To accommodate more soldiers
b) To prevent mining
c) For defence

Parts of the Castle

A castle had one or more courtyards, with main rooms in buildings along the insides of the courtyard walls. Near the great hall, where everyone ate, were the pantry and kitchen. Stables, workshops and extra living rooms were located in wall towers or in buildings separate from the great hall.

Where were the stables?

Stables were usually built in one of the castle courtyards. Like many buildings inside the walls, they could be large but were often built of timber. Near the stables was a workshop for the farrier, the craftsman who made and fitted horseshoes.

What was in a keep?

As the keep was one of the strongest parts of the castle, everything of value was kept in its basement. The lord's hall was above this, with the family's private rooms on the upper floor. Further floors were used by members of the lord's household.

Were dungeons really prisons?

The basement rooms in castle towers, now called dungeons, were storerooms, not prisons. Weapons, equipment and food would be kept here. Prisons were rare in the Middle Ages and the only people held prisoner for long periods were nobles captured in battle. These people could then be set free in return for money (right) from their families.

Where was the bathroom?

Castles did not have bathrooms like those in modern houses! When people washed they used a bowl of water. For toilets there were garderobes. A garderobe consisted of a wooden seat above a stone drain which emptied through the castle wall directly into the moat. Garderobes were smelly and must have been cold, as the drain usually led straight out into the open air.

How was the food cooked?

Castles had no modern kitchen appliances, so most food was cooked over the fire (left). The cook roasted meat on a spit, which could be turned with a handle so that the food was cooked all round. Other foods were boiled in a large iron pot over the flames. Castle kitchens also had ovens for baking the bread that everyone ate with their meals.

Quick-fire Quiz

1. What was in the keep basement?
a) The hall
b) The storeroom
c) The kitchen

2. What did a farrier make?
a) Castles
b) Horseshoes
c) Bread

3. When might you be imprisoned?
a) For a minor crime
b) For a serious crime
c) For ransom

4. Why were garderobes cold?
a) They were used only in winter
b) They drained into the open air
c) They had large windows

How were wall towers used?

Wall towers (left) were used in all kinds of ways. Guards could get the best view of the surrounding country from the top of the stair turret, and could fire at an enemy from the battlements around the roof. In the rooms below, there were more windows to shoot out from. In peacetime, these rooms, which often had fireplaces, provided accommodation for the soldiers or members of the lord's family.

Did castles have gardens?

Many castles had gardens where vegetables and herbs were grown for cooking. In the later Middle Ages, when castles became more luxurious, some even had ornamental gardens. Here the flowers, herbs, shrubs and trees were arranged in neat patterns.

Castle Life

During peacetime, the lord and his followers collected rent from tenants and made sure the castle was in good repair. Knights went hunting to bring extra food for the table. Women and girls spun wool, cooked, and mended clothes. In the evening, everyone came together for a meal in the great hall.

Where did everyone sleep?

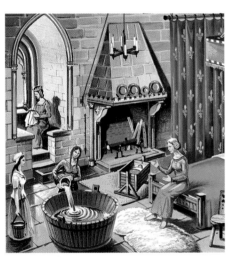

Medieval castles had no bedrooms. The lord and his family usually slept in the solar (right), a private room next to the hall. Most of the rest of the household slept in the hall itself. After the evening meal, they took down the tables and leaned them against the wall, and put straw-filled mattresses on the floor. Others slept where they worked. Cooks, for example, slept in the kitchen.

What was on the menu?

People ate whatever farmers could provide – plus what could be hunted. If food was plentiful, the diet included meat such as venison and boar together with beef, pork and mutton from the farm. Bread and vegetables were served with the meat, often on a *trencher* – a dinner plate of firm bread. This was washed down with ale or wine (right). In lean times, people ate meat preserved with salt and flavoured with herbs to hide the salty taste.

Trencher

What sort of music entertained the guests?

Minstrels (right) played instruments and sang songs. The fiddle was popular but after the crusades, many minstrels took up an Arab instrument, the lute. In Wales, musicians played the harp, while the harp-like psaltery was played all over Europe.

Did women have rights?

Medieval women had few rights. Few were educated and most had to endure a life of household chores. If a woman had property, it passed to her husband when she died. For the lady of the manor, things could be different. She helped run the manor if her husband was away, and might even have to defend the castle.

Who was the boss?

The lord was the boss, and everyone had to obey him. His power covered almost every aspect of life, from how his land should be farmed to who rode into battle with him. The only area that the lord did not control was religion, when his power was second to that of the local bishop and clergy.

Who helped the lord?

A host of servants, from the steward to the reeve, helped run the lord's manor (see page 30). Others performed menial duties in the castle (above). Pages served at the lord's table while grooms looked after his horses. He might have a clerk – who could also be the chaplain – to keep records and write letters. But the lord's constant companion and most important personal servant was his squire (see pages 14–15).

(see page 30)
(see pages 14–15)

How did people keep warm?

Compared with houses today, castles and manor houses were cold and draughty, even when heated with blazing log fires. To keep down the draughts, the lords lined their walls with tapestries. People wore several layers of thick woollen clothing in the winter, and the rich added garments trimmed with fur (right) when the weather was really cold.

Becoming a Knight

To become a knight, a young man had to belong to a noble family. As a boy, he began his training as a page and learned how to behave in a noble household. As a teenager, he became a squire – learning knightly conduct and how to handle weapons and horses. Finally, in a ceremony known as dubbing, he became a knight.

Serving at table

Practising with a lance

How did you become a page?

If you were the son of a noble family, you did not go to school. Instead, when you were about seven years old, you were sent away to be a page in the household of another lord. Here you learned good manners and such skills as carrying food to the table (right), and serving your lord and lady.

What did a squire do?

A squire was a knight's personal servant and helper. His duties included looking after all the weapons and tending the horses. Before a battle the squire helped his master put on armour. He may even have had to fight beside his lord, providing aid if the knight was wounded. By doing all these things, a squire learned how to behave as a knight.

Did knights pray?

In the Middle Ages, religion played a big part in most people's lives. When a squire was to be made a knight, he often spent the whole night before the dubbing ceremony at prayer in the castle chapel (left). This vigil was a sign that he would take his vows seriously to serve his king faithfully for the rest of his life.

How did squires practise sword play?

For practice, knights and squires often used a sword and a small round shield called a buckler. To build up strength, squires were sometimes given swords that were heavier than those actually used in battle. Pages or young squires might even be given wooden swords with which to practise.

Exercising

Helping the knight

Practising swordplay

Dubbing

How did squires exercise muscles?

Squires kept fit by practising sword play, wrestling, throwing the javelin, and all sorts of other sporting activities. They made sure that they were fit in case they had to go into battle.

Were knights and squires well mannered?

Knights and squires were supposed to behave with good manners. They were meant to be considerate to women and courteous to all. But they did not always live up to this ideal. Sometimes squires got together in rowdy gangs and went around causing mischief. On one occasion they even burned down part of a town.

What was dubbing?

Dubbing was the ceremony at which a squire was made into a knight. The squire kneeled in front of his lord or the king, who tapped him on the shoulder with his sword. The new knight was then presented with a sword and spurs. There was often a celebration afterwards.

15

Heraldry

In the Middle Ages every noble family had a coat of arms that acted as its badge. A knight wore his coat of arms into battle and when competing in a tournament so that he could be easily recognized. Coats of arms were always designed in a similar way, using the same range of colours and basic patterns.

Groom's arms

Bride's arms

Combined coat of arms

How was a coat of arms designed?

The herald chose the colours, shapes and other designs that were suitable for the family who were to bear the arms. He made sure that the design was different to all others – every coat of arms had to be unique. When two noble families were united by marriage, the couple could have their two coats of arms combined (above), with the bride's and groom's arms on opposite sides of the shield.

What did heraldic symbols mean?

Many of the symbols used in heraldry have special meanings. Designs such as the diagonal bar (left) showed that the bearer's parents were not married. This was important in the Middle Ages as an illegitimate son would not be able to inherit his father's title or lands.

What were a herald's duties?

A herald was an officer in the household of the king or great lord. As well as designing coats of arms (above), it was his job to organize ceremonies and tournaments. In war, the herald carried messages between opposing armies (left). Therefore, it was essential that he could recognize every coat of arms, and so deliver the message to the right person.

How could you recognize an eldest son?

An eldest son used his father's coat of arms but with an added element. While the father was alive, the son's coat of arms were marked with a symbol called a label. The label ran across the shoulders and looked like a horizontal line with three thicker downward-pointing lines joined to it. When the father died, the eldest son removed the label.

How were knights identified on the battlefield?

A knight's shield and his surcoat – a loose robe worn over the armour – were decorated with his coat of arms. This made it easy to see who was who in the confusion of battle. Heralds also used coats of arms to identify casualties after the battle (below).

Quick-fire Quiz

1. Which of these was a herald's job?
a) Carrying messages
b) Fighting
c) Looking after the horses

2. Where were the supporters placed?
a) Above the shield
b) Below the shield
c) On either side of the shield

3. What was red called in heraldry?
a) Or
b) Scarlet
c) Gules

4. What mark denoted an eldest son?
a) Bar
b) Label
c) Chevron

What was the language of heraldry?

Coats of arms were described in a special language based on Old French. Each of the colours has its own name in this language, for example red was called gules and black was referred to as sable. Experts on heraldry still use this language to describe coats of arms today.

What were supporters?

The supporters were a pair of figures that stood either side of the shield in a coat of arms, as if they were holding it up. These figures were often animals and could be real beasts, such as lions or antelopes, or mythical ones, such as unicorns or griffons. Supporters were not normally shown on a knight's surcoat, but were included in the full coat of arms.

Horsemanship

Whether fighting, hunting or travelling, a knight spent much of his time on horseback. A horse was the knight's most valued possession. As a page or squire, he was shown how to ride and how to care for his mount. As he got older, he learned how to fight on horseback using a sword and lance so that he could fight for his king and take part in tournaments.

How many horses did a knight own?

Most knights had several horses, which were used for different tasks. A knight would have one or two warhorses (destriers) together with a powerful horse for hunting (a courser) and perhaps another animal for travelling. Knights also kept packhorses in their stables. These were used to carry luggage when the knight and his household were travelling or when items had to be sent across country.

What was a destrier?

Destrier was the usual name for a warhorse. Destriers were large, powerful stallions that could carry their owners swiftly into battle. The best and costliest destriers were said to come from southern Europe, especially from Italy and Spain. The name destrier comes from the Latin word for right, perhaps because the horse led with its right leg, swerving away from an opponent in battle.

How could you stop a horse in its tracks?

If footsoldiers were going into battle against mounted knights, they might scatter fearsome looking spiked objects called caltrops on the ground. A caltrop had four metal spikes, and these were arranged so that whichever way the caltrop landed, one spike pointed upwards. A caltrop could injure a horse that stepped on it.

Caltrop

How did a knight control his horse?

A knight controlled his horse with both his feet and his hands. He placed his feet in a pair of stirrups, and used them to grip his mount. This meant that the knight's hands were free to hold the reins or wield a sword or lance. The leather reins were connected to a bit that was placed in the horse's mouth. By changing the tension of the reins, the knight could make his horse speed up (right), slow down, or turn a corner.

Stirrup

Were spurs cruel?

A good rider would use his spurs only sparingly, for example when urging his horse to give an extra turn of speed. Even so, a jab from the single long metal spike of a prick spur must have hurt; rowel spurs, with their rings of shorter spikes, did less damage.

Rowel spur

Armoured horse

How could a knight protect his horse?

Some knights had armour made for their warhorses because it was just as dangerous for a horse in battle as it was for the animal's rider. Horse armour was usually made up of a shaffron, or head-piece, and a crinet, a series of metal plates that covered the neck. Because plate armour was expensive, the rest of the horse sometimes went unprotected into battle.

Quick-fire Quiz

1. A prick spur had how many spikes?
a) One
b) Two
c) Three

2. What was a caltrop used for?
a) Killing soldiers
b) Controlling horses
c) Injuring horses

3. Where were the best war horses bred?
a) Holland and Germany
b) Spain and Italy
c) Britain and Ireland

4. What was a knight's most valued possession?
a) His sword
b) His horse
c) His armour

Weapons and Fighting

The most feared sight on a medieval battlefield was a line of enemy knights charging directly at you. Well armoured, mounted on warhorses and wielding weapons that they had spent years training to use, knights were fast, powerful and difficult to stop. A knight's favourite weapon was the sword, which could be used either on foot or from a horse, but he was adept with other weapons.

How did the Normans use their shields?

Norman soldiers held their large, kite-shaped shields in front of them to give plenty of protection. If a group of men were fighting in a row, they moved their shields together (below), to form a wall that archers or even mounted warriors found difficult to break through.

What was a double-edged sword used for?

A two-edged sword was used for cutting and slashing blows. This type of weapon was very effective against an enemy who was not wearing armour, especially if it was a 'great sword' with a large grip that the knight could hold in both hands. He could then use all his strength to deliver powerful, cutting blows.

Mace
Shield
Sword
Dagger
Crossbow
Battle-axe
Arrows
Longbow

Did knights use only swords and daggers?

In addition to the sword, the knight used several other hand weapons (above and right) including the battle-axe and the mace. The mace was especially fearsome because its raised metal ridges or spikes concentrated the power of the blow, knocking the enemy sideways.

How did you use a flail?

A flail consisted of a wooden handle linked by a chain to a spiked metal ball. A knight normally used the flail when fighting on foot. He aimed to strike at an enemy's head, knocking him out or piercing his armour.

How could you injure someone who was wearing mail?

To do serious injury to an opponent in mail, a knight needed a sword or dagger with a narrow, sharp point, to get through one of the gaps between the metal rings. Archers (right) also found that they could pierce mail by using narrow metal heads on their arrows.

When was a lance used?

A lance was a long, heavy weapon like a pole, which was most effective at the start of a battle. Wielded by mounted knights charging at speed, it could kill a man with a single thrust. After the charge, the knight discarded the lance and drew his sword – a better weapon for close-quarters fighting.

How were swords made stronger?

Armourers gave blades extra strength by altering their shape. A blade with a cross-section like an elongated diamond was the strongest. Both cutting and stabbing swords (below) were made with blades in this shape.

Quick-fire Quiz

1. How did you hold a great sword?
a) Close to the chest
b) With one hand
c) With two hands

2 Which blade shape gave greatest strength?
a) Diamond
b) Rounded
c) Hollow

3. What did a weapon need to pierce mail?
a) A narrow point
b) Extra power
c) Plenty of weight

4. Where was a knight most likely to use a flail?
a) On horseback
b) On foot
c) In a boat

21

Armour

Every knight wanted to go into battle well protected. In the early Middle Ages, knights wore mail, but armour made up of metal plates became more popular. Knights liked plate armour because it protected them well from arrows and sword blows, while allowing them to move with great freedom. But only a rich man could afford a full suit of plate armour.

How could you 'knit' with metal?

By making mail! Mail, or chain mail as it is sometimes called, was a form of armour made up of thousands of tiny linked metal rings. By varying the number of rings in a row, the armourer could shape mail into garments such as shirts, head-coverings, leg-guards, and even mittens. Mail was popular until plate armour became fashionable in the late thirteenth century.

Single ring

Linked mail

What did the armourer do?

Armourers (below) were skilled craftsmen who made both armour and weapons and could beat pieces of metal into sturdy breastplates or helmets. They did this by hammering a sheet of metal on an anvil or on a rounded object called a former. This gave the piece the right curve. Suits of armour often came back damaged from battle, so armourers also spent a lot of time on repairs.

Conical helmet

Basinet

Great helm (jousting)

Frog-mouthed (jousting)

Barbute

Why were there so many types of helmet?

Fashions in helmets changed just like fashions in clothes. Late fourteenth-century knights often wore the basinet, a helmet with a pointed visor and a collar of mail, which offered excellent protection. By the mid-fifteenth century, they were wearing lighter helmets, called barbutes. For jousts and tournaments, a rich knight might wear a highly decorated great helm.

What did a knight wear under his armour?

Under his armour a knight wore a padded jacket called an arming doublet. The doublet had sections of mail sewn under the arms and in other places to protect areas where there were gaps between the plates.

Helmet

Bevor

Breastplate

Was plate armour heavy?

Plate armour was the strongest armour of all. It looks very heavy, but a full suit weighed little more than 20 kilograms. This compared well with mail, because a mail shirt alone could weigh 14 kilograms, and when a helmet and mail leg-guards were added, the suit could weigh more than a suit of plates. A knight in plate armour could move about or mount a horse with ease.

Plate armour

Pauldron

Besagew

How was plate armour attached to the body?

Some of the sections were tied to the leather thongs on the padded undergarment. The other pieces were attached with leather straps and buckles, which fitted around the knight's legs or waist. A knight needed his squire to help with the tricky business of attaching all the plates.

Tasset

Vambrace

Gauntlet

Cuisse

How could the plates move?

Many of the main sections of a suit of plate armour, such as the part protecting the arm, were made up of several smaller pieces of metal (below). These small pieces were joined together by flexible leather links or sliding rivets, so that they could move backwards and forwards. This gave the knight lots of freedom of movement as he walked, rode, and fought.

Greave

Sabaton

Quick-fire Quiz

1. Which was the strongest armour?
a) Plate
b) Mail
c) Leather

2. What was an arming doublet?
a) A helmet
b) A padded jacket
c) A coat of mail

3. How were plate sections fixed together?
a) By welding
b) With chains
c) With leather thongs and rivets

4. A popular 14th century helmet was called a...?
a) Barbute
b) Basinet
c) Great helm

Siege

When an enemy arrived in force to attack a castle, the castle's owner and his men pulled up the drawbridge and got ready for a siege. The siege could end peacefully, especially if the defenders ran out of food and were forced to surrender. But if there was a fight, the attackers could use all sorts of powerful weapons to force their way in.

How effective were archers?

The longbow was one of the medieval soldier's most awesome weapons. Its deadly arrows could fly some 300m and a skilled archer could fire up to 12 arrows per minute. Castle defenders were forced to hide behind the battlements to avoid the arrows' sharp metal points.

What were siege engines?

The devices used by medieval armies to attack castles were known as siege engines. These were fearsome weapons for hurling missiles at the enemy or knocking down walls. The trebuchet and mangonel were catapults powerful enough to fling rocks. The ballista, a giant crossbow, shot bolts that were often tipped with blazing rags. Weapons on wheeled platforms could be moved into position to find their target. Reloading very large devices was slow work, but their devastating power struck fear into the enemy.

How could an attacker get through walls?

One way was to batter down the walls using a ram, a huge tree trunk mounted on wheels. A group of men, protected by the ram's roof, pushed the weapon repeatedly at the walls. Alternatively, attackers could try wheeling a wooden siege tower up to the walls and climbing over. Both ram and tower were covered with animal skins to protect their wooden structures from flaming arrows.

Siege tower

Ram

What was mining and how was it done?

Mining was another way of bringing down castle walls. The miners dug a tunnel under the walls, holding everything up with wooden props. Once they had finished digging, they lit a fire in the tunnel. This set the props alight, so that the walls above no longer had anything to support them. If all went according to plan, a section of the castle walls collapsed and the attackers swarmed into the castle. If the defenders could see a mine being dug, they could retaliate by digging their own tunnel into the mine and fighting off the attackers.

Tunnel entrance far outside the walls

Miners set fire to wooden props

Workers bring wood for the fire

Removing vital foundation rocks

Trebuchet

How did a catapult work?

Catapults worked like giant slings to launch missiles. Trebuchets used counterweights; the mangonel's sling was held in place by ropes, which were then released. It took many men to reload the largest catapults.

Quick-fire Quiz

1. What were siege towers covered in?
a) Wood
b) Animal skins
c) Turf

2. How fast could an archer shoot?
a) 2 times a minute
b) 12 times a minute
c) 22 times a minute

3. How did miners hold up a tunnel?
a) With stone pillars
b) With their hands
c) With wood props

4. What was a trebuchet for?
a) To enable attackers to scale walls
b) To fling rocks over and at castle walls
c) To spy into an enemy castle

Defence

Everything about a castle was designed to make it easy to defend. The walls were thick to withstand attacks from siege engines, while windows were small to keep out arrows. Battlements, towers and hoardings all gave good lines of fire.

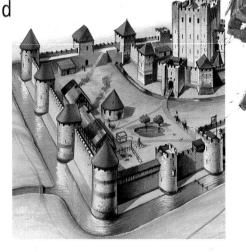

What was a moat?

A moat was a barrier between the castle and its attackers. Many castles were surrounded by dry ditches, but a water-filled moat gave more protection. An attacker could walk across a dry ditch and start mining – digging holes under the walls to make them fall down. With a moat, it was virtually impossible for the enemy to undermine the castle walls.

What were murder holes?

Murder holes were small openings in the ceiling, usually within a castle gatehouse. They enabled defenders to look down on anyone passing through the gate below. If the person below was an enemy, the defender could shoot arrows or pour boiling liquid through one of the holes.

How was an embrasure used?

An embrasure was a hole in the wall where an archer could stand. The hole was splayed on the inside, so that the archer could stand to one side of the opening, out of reach of enemy fire. When the archer was ready to shoot, he moved quickly to the opening, fired his arrow, and then ducked back out of range.

How could you pour boiling oil on your enemies?

Castle defenders sometimes emptied boiling oil or water straight over the battlements on to their enemies below. Another method was to use the machicolations, which were holes in the floor right next to the battlements. Anything poured through these would land on an opponent who was attacking the base of the wall or trying to climb it.

How did you make a sortie?

To make a sortie (left), defenders left the safety of the castle and launched an attack on the besieging enemy. The defenders would burst out, trying to take their enemies by surprise before the walls of their stronghold were destroyed. A sortie would often target the powerful siege engines and their trained crews.

What were hoardings?

Wooden hoardings (right) were often built over the battlements to protect archers while providing them with a wide field of fire. Sometimes hoardings also had holes in the floor, for pouring boiling oil or firing at attackers directly below.

What was a portcullis?

A portcullis was a barred gate controlled by ropes and pulleys. It was closed by dropping it down from above. If a portcullis was dropped down on an enemy, he could be caught between its spiked bars (right).

Quick-fire Quiz

1. Where would you find murder holes?
a) In the walls
b) In the ceiling
c) In the battlements

2. How were machicolations used?
a) For ventilation
b) For letting in light
c) For pouring boiling oil onto attackers

3. Hoardings were made from...
a) Wood
b) Leather
c) Stone

4. What could a moat prevent?
a) Mining
b) Arrows
c) Siege engines

27

The Crusades

In the late eleventh century, Christian rulers tried to take control of the Holy Land – the part of the Middle East where Jesus had lived. At that time, the Holy Land was ruled by the Muslims – followers of Islam – to whom the area was also sacred. It was the start of a bitter conflict – the Crusades.

Who went on the Crusades?

All sorts of people went on the Crusades. Some were kings, such as Richard I of England and Philip II of France. Others were nobles, and many were men-at-arms who went with their lords to the east. A large number of poor peasants also went on crusade, inspired by leaders such as the French monk Peter the Hermit.

Why did they go?

Many crusaders were men who genuinely believed that it was right to fight for control of the Christian sites in the Holy Land (right). But others went just for the adventure or because they thought that they could benefit themselves, either by looting after battles or by setting themselves up as lords in the east. Many of the latter were the younger sons of nobles, who would not inherit any of their parents' wealth back home.

What was the Children's Crusade?

In 1212, Nicholas, a 12-year-old boy from Cologne, Germany, led thousands of children across the Alps and into Italy on their way to the Holy Land. Another boy, Stephen, from France, led a further group of children. Both groups failed. Stephen and his followers were captured and sold as slaves, the followers of Nicholas died in Italy.

Who were the 'fighting monks'?

The fighting monks were groups of men who took religious vows but were still allowed to fight the Muslims. There were several groups, or orders, of fighting monks – the Knights Templar (named after their headquarters near the Temple in Jerusalem), the Knights of St John (famous for their work healing the sick), and the Teutonic Knights (who originally came from Germany).

What did the crusades achieve?

Although the crusaders set up states in the Middle East, these were soon reconquered. Only the ruins of their great castles, such as Krak des Chevaliers (below), survive. But they brought useful knowledge back to Europe as well as new medicines and eastern inventions such as the windmill.

Who was Saladin?

Saladin was a twelfth-century Muslim leader who ruled Egypt and part of Syria. He defended his lands from crusaders and defeated the Second Crusade. When the Third Crusade began, Saladin fought Richard I of England. Again Saladin was victorious, and greatly reduced the crusaders' power.

Saladin

How many Crusades were there?

There were eight separate Crusades from Europe to the Holy Land between the eleventh and thirteenth centuries. The most successful was the first (1096–99), which was led by a group of French and Norman barons. It ended with the capture of Jerusalem. In 1271, the last crusader territory in the Holy Land was lost to the Muslims.

Quick-fire Quiz

1. Which French king led a crusade?
a) Philip I
b) Philip II
c) Richard I

2. Who led the First Crusade?
a) French and Norman barons
b) Richard I
c) German lords

3. Which was the most successful crusade?
a) The fourth
b) The second
c) The first

4. What were the Knights of St John known for?
a) Healing the sick
b) Helping the poor
c) Fighting for St John

The Knight's Manor

A manor consisted of a lord's castle, church, houses for the peasants and farmland. The lord was the most important person. He was the landlord, boss and judge, and the peasants had to do what he told them. These peasants were known as serfs or villeins; they had no freedom.

Who looked after the money?

The person who kept the accounts on the manor was the steward (left). He had to be educated, although most accounting systems were primitive. Later, a group of merchants in Italy invented the system of 'double-entry' book-keeping, which is still used by accountants today. As well as looking after the money, the steward managed the lord's farm, and also acted as judge in the manorial court if the lord was away.

What did the bailiff do?

The bailiff was a peasant farmer who had his own land. As well as his own fields, he looked after the day-to-day running of the lord's personal land, making sure that all the jobs were done properly and at the right time. In addition, the bailiff was responsible for repairs and building work on the manor, bringing in any workers, such as stone masons or carpenters, to get these jobs done. He was second in importance to the steward.

What was life like for the workers?

Life was hard for peasants. Men spent nearly all their time working in the fields. Women had to cook, look after the house and make the family's clothes. For children there was no school. Boys helped in the fields while girls learned how to spin, sew and cook. Sunday and religious holidays were the only days off. For some, local markets (below) offered a welcome break from the hardships of daily life.

Who kept watch on the peasants?

The reeve (right) was the person who kept an eye on the peasants. He was a peasant himself, chosen by his peers, and he worked closely with the bailiff. He was most often seen out in the fields, making sure that everyone was working hard. But if any of the workers had a problem, the reeve could tell the bailiff, who would then decide what to do, or whether to report the matter to the lord.

Reeve

Who worked the lord's land?

The lord's land was divided into two sections. Most was allotted to the peasants who worked the land in return for services to the lord and a share of the produce. The rest of the lord's land was called the demesne. This was farmed by the lord with the help of the peasants, who owed him some of their labour each week.

Who dealt with criminals?

The lord held his own court in his hall for minor crimes. Punishments included whipping, beating, fines or being locked in the stocks. Serious offences were judged by the county sheriff and could be punished by death by hanging. The church had its own laws and courts (above) for dealing with law-breakers among the clergy.

What happened when people were ill?

Medieval medicine was basic. Some herbal medicines worked well, but other remedies, such as blood-letting, did no good. As a result, many people died of minor illnesses, and few lived beyond the age of 40. Life was especially hard for women, many of whom died in childbirth. The most feared illness was bubonic plague or the Black Death (right). It killed a third of the population of Europe in the mid-fourteenth century.

Quick-fire Quiz

1. Who was judge in the court when the lord was away?
a) The bailiff
b) The reeve
c) The steward

2. Who farmed the demesne?
a) The lord
b) The sheriff
c) The reeve

3. How many years did a peasant spend at school?
a) 10
b) 6
c) None

4. What caused so many women to die young?
a) Overwork
b) The Black Death
c) Childbirth

Peacetime Pursuits

In the Middle Ages, people had to make their own entertainment. Poor families filled their limited spare time with simple games and story-telling. For noble families, life was easier, but even knights had to mix some of their pleasure with work. Many liked to hunt, but the main reason for hunting was to provide food.

What was chivalry?

Chivalry was a code of conduct that all knights were meant to follow. A knight was expected to be considerate, especially towards women, and to treat enemies with respect. Many did not live up to this, but the Middle Ages are often known as the 'Age of Chivalry'.

What were the favourite games?

Peasant children usually played games, such as leapfrog and tag, that did not need any equipment, since ordinary families could not afford toys. Noble families had more money, and a knight's children were sometimes given toys, such as wooden swords and shields, or miniature models of men-at-arms.

What about pastimes for adults?

Some people liked to play board games, such as chess (above), which appealed to noblemen because chess is like a battle. Otherwise, knights and their ladies looked forward to visits from musicians and actors who arrived from time to time and performed in return for board and lodging.

How did a falconer exercise his birds?

Falconers trained their birds to hunt and bring back prey. One way to exercise a falcon was to let it hunt for animals as it would in the wild. An alternative was to use a lure – a dummy bird on the end of a long string. The falconer twirled the lure around in the air, encouraging the bird to pounce on to it.

Why did girls learn to spin?

In the Middle Ages most manors kept sheep for meat and also for wool. It was the job of the women and girls to spin the wool into yarn, which was then woven into cloth. A simple spindle or wooden spinning wheel was all that was needed, so almost every medieval girl learned to spin to produce yarn.

How did people like to be entertained?

One of the favourite pastimes was telling stories. Few people could read, but popular tales were handed down from one generation to the next by word of mouth. People liked to listen to stories about the exploits and loves of knights in times gone by. Some of the favourites were about the adventures of the mythical English king, Arthur (right), and his knights of the round table.

Which creatures did knights most enjoy hunting?

Knights hunted animals that they could eat. They liked best to chase large creatures that provided plenty of meat – and offered a challenge to the hunter. Deer and wild boar were favourites. When these animals were scarce, smaller creatures like hares were hunted. Poorer people might hunt birds or rabbits. In the Middle Ages, there were few imported foods, and everyone had to eat what could be grown on the local land. So hunting made the diet more varied. Hunting also offered knights useful riding practice for war.

Quick-fire Quiz

1. What animals did knights hunt?
a) Falcons
b) Dogs
c) Deer

2. Which king was a favourite of storytellers?
a) King Alfred
b) King Arthur
c) King Albert

3. What are the Middle Ages sometimes called?
a) Age of Innocence
b) Age of Chivalry
c) Bronze Age

4. Which board game was popular with noblemen?
a) Chess
b) Drafts
c) Solitaire

Tournaments

Knights needed to practise fighting, so they often engaged in mock combat as a rehearsal for war. Many people liked to watch the knights fighting, so tournaments soon became great festivals to which spectators came from far afield. As well as mock-battles, knights also fought one-to-one on horseback in the joust and with swords in foot combat.

How was jousting done?

In a joust (right), two mounted knights hurtled towards each other and tried to knock one another off their horses as they passed. The weapon they used was the lance – either a pointed lance for the 'joust of war', or a safer, blunt lance for the 'joust of peace'. Both types of joust were stunning spectacles. Knights wore special armour for the joust. Their breastplates had metal rests for their lances, and they wore helmets that covered the entire head. Only a narrow slit was left in the helmet to allow the knight to see his target.

How did squires practise for the joust?

Jousting was dangerous, so knights invented a safer way for themselves and their squires to practise. They rode towards the quintain, a device with two moving arms attached to a wooden post. One arm held a shield, the other a heavy weight. The squire had to hit the shield with his lance and then ride past at speed to avoid being hit by the swinging weight, which would be spinning quickly round towards him.

What if you weren't a knight?

If you were not a knight you could train for war by practising archery. Archers organised competitions, with everyone trying to hit the gold disc at the centre of the target. To protect others, there was a barrier or mound of earth – the butts – behind the targets.

What drew spectators to the tournament?

Many people liked the pageantry seen at the tournament. This included the knights' shields decorated with their coats of arms, the banners, and the brightly patterned cloths – known as caparisons – on the horses. As the knights rode through the streets to the tournament, onlookers could easily recognize those they supported from all the badges and heraldry.

Who took part in tournaments?

It was mostly knights who took part, and they were usually members of the country's powerful families. Large-scale mock-battles, called mêlées, (right) involved many knights and sometimes also foot soldiers. Tournaments were hosted by the king or one of his highest-ranking lords. As well as giving battle practice, tournaments showed people how strong the king was and how many knightly followers he had.

35

The Last Castles

After the fifteenth century, nobles stopped building castles as secure strongholds. Instead, they built elegant houses in which to enjoy a life of comfort. This came about because of changes in the way nobles lived and how battles were fought. Some families still lived in buildings that looked like castles from the outside, but would have been of little use in war.

Were cannons effective against castles?

The first cannons (above), used from the fourteenth century onwards, did not always work very well. They made lots of noise, but damaged few castles. But as time went on, cannons became larger and more reliable and could blow huge holes in castle walls. This meant that, by the sixteenth century, castles were no longer as secure from attack as they had been.

Was armour bullet-proof?

Yes. Armourers normally tried to make their plates thick enough to stop a bullet. As firearms became more common from the fifteenth century onwards, people were anxious to be protected by their armour. So armourers often fired bullets at their breastplates before they left the workshop. The mark left by the bullet reassured the wearer that he would be safe.

How did leather replace armour?

By the seventeenth century, light cavalry soldiers (left) were doing the jobs of knights on the battlefield. Many of these horsemen found that a jerkin of pale leather – called a buff *coat* – gave them enough protection from sword cuts. Buff coats were worn with a metal breastplate and helmet, to shield the most vulnerable parts of the body.

Why did knights stop building castles?

In 1453, the Ottoman Turks laid siege to Constantinople (modern Istanbul), the capital of the Byzantine Empire (left). When their firearms battered down the walls and the Turks swarmed into the great city, it seemed to be the end of an era. Lords realised that there was little point in building stone castles for defence. At the same time, the feudal system was breaking down. Knights were no longer powerful and other people – especially merchants – were getting richer. The age of castles was at an end.

Are there 'new' castles?

Many nobles in the late eighteenth and nineteenth centuries wanted to revive the Age of Chivalry. They designed their homes in the style of castles by adding towers, gatehouses, thick walls and pointed windows, to create buildings like Schloss Neuschwanstein in Germany (above).

Why are so many castles ruined?

A castle could be damaged in a siege, and 'slighted' by an enemy to make it unusable. Some lords abandoned their castles because they wanted a more comfortable home. Local people would use much of the stone to build new houses.

How did castles change?

Lords still lived in castles after the fifteenth century, but these castles were no longer built to withstand a siege. Nobles added features that gave them more comfort, such as luxurious bedrooms. Inside walls were lined with wooden panelling and decorated plasterwork adorned the ceilings. Castle owners also put in bigger windows, so that the rooms were much more light and airy than in medieval castles.

Timeline

This timeline records the key dates in the history of castles and knights. Most of the story takes place in a period known as the Middle Ages, or the medieval era. This period is called the 'Middle' Ages because it is midway between the end of the Roman Empire (in the fifth century) and the Renaissance (in the fifteenth century). The period does not have precise dates, but many historians say that the Middle Ages lasted from 500 to 1500.

AD1 to AD800

1–500 Romans use light cavalry troops to support footsoldiers. They build forts throughout Europe to defend their empire.

350–550 Western Roman Empire disintegrates.

410 Goths sack Rome.

622 The Islamic religion is established.

634 Omar I, caliph of the Arab Muslims, conquers Holy Land from Byzantines.

771 Charlemagne becomes king of the Franks. He uses mounted warriors to defend his lands.

790s Vikings begin raids on Britain and mainland Europe.

AD800 to AD1000

800 Charlemagne is crowned Holy Roman Emperor by Pope Leo III.

800–1000 Rulers in western Europe begin to grant land to their nobles in return for services – the feudal system is established.

800–1150 The current style of architecture is the Romanesque, featuring rounded arches, thick walls, and tunnel-like barrel vaults.

911 The Viking leader Rollo settles with his followers in northwestern France. They become known as the Normans and their territory Normandy.

950 The stone keep at Doué-la-Fontaine, France, is built. This is now the oldest stone keep to survive.

987–1040 Foulques Nerra of Anjou builds 27 castles as part of his war with the Count of Blois.

AD1000 to AD1100

1000 The Normans spread the fashion for castle-building around many areas of Europe. They begin by building wooden motte-and-bailey castles but later construct castles using stone.

1000–1200 Many Italian towns become independent states, each defended with its own stone walls and castle. Italian lords each build their own stone tower, and some cities have many towers, with lords competing to build the tallest.

1066 William of Normandy invades England and defeats King Harold II at the Battle of Hastings. As his nobles take over, they build castles all over the country to increase their power.

1071 William of Poitiers, said to be the first troubadour (medieval poet and singer), is born.

1090 Christian writers lay down rules of conduct for knights. The rules become the code of chivalry.

1095 Pope Urban II preaches the First Crusade.

1096–1099 The First Crusade. Jerusalem is captured from the Muslims.

1100 Tower keeps become popular in many areas. In England and France, stocky, square towers are common; German knights prefer more slender towers surrounded by strong curtain walls.

AD1100 to AD1200

1100–1200 Many crusader castles are built.

1113 The Knights of St John are founded in Jerusalem.

1118 The Knights Templar build their first headquarters near the Temple in Jerusalem.

1142 Crusaders take and rebuild Syria's greatest castle, the Krak des Chevaliers.

1147–49 The Second Crusade.

1150 The Gothic style replaces the Romaneqsue as the favoured building style.

1160 Castle builders experiment with different shaped keeps. Round keeps and many-sided designs are tried.

1170 Many Norman mottes with wooden towers are converted into stone shell keeps.

1180 Philip Augustus, one of the greatest French kings, comes to the throne; he will build many castles in his kingdom.

1188–92 The Third Crusade.

1190 The Teutonic Knights are founded. They build many castles in Europe.

1190 The keep goes out of fashion. Builders concentrate on courtyard castles with strong gatehouses.

1196 Richard I begins work on Château Gaillard, France. One of the strongest castles, it will withstand a siege for over a year.

AD1200 to AD1300

1200 Rounded wall towers become popular.

1202–04 The Fourth Crusade.

1212 The Children's Crusade.

1217–22 The Fifth Crusade.

1228–29 The Sixth Crusade.

1220 Frederick II, one of the greatest castle builders, becomes Holy Roman Emperor.

1248–54 The Seventh Crusade.

1270 Rise of the concentric castle.

1270 The Eighth Crusade.

1272 Edward I comes to the throne of England. He launches military campaigns against the Scots and Welsh, and builds many castles to control the population.

1291 Sultan Baybars storms the Christian city of Acre, and the crusading movement comes to an end.

AD1300 to AD1400

1302 Battle of Courtrai. Flemish peasants armed with pikes defeat mounted French knights, proving that knights are not invincible in battle.

1312 The Knights Templar are dissolved.

1320s Cannons are first used in Europe.

1330 Plate armour becomes more fashionable.

1337–1453 The Hundred Years' War between England and France.

1347–51 The Black Death kills around one third of the population of Europe.

1380 Castle builders start to use gun loops, so that defenders can fire out safely.

AD1400 to AD1600

1400 Decline of castles begins.

1415 Battle of Agincourt. Henry V of England defeats army of French knights.

1450 Thicker walls are built to protect castles from pounding by cannon.

1453 The city of Constantinople, capital of the Byzantine Empire, falls to the Ottoman Turks, ending the Byzantine Empire.

1476–7 France fights wars with the Duchy of Burgundy; the widespread use of pikes and hand guns shows that the age of the knight is coming to an end.

1500s Lords convert their castles into more comfortable residences or build palaces.

1509 Henry VIII builds forts (strongholds designed for guns where no one lives permanently) rather than true castles.

AD1600 to AD2000

1650 Star-shaped forts used to defend many towns in France.

1800 People begin to be interested in castles as symbols of the 'Age of Chivalry'.

1854 French architect Eugène-Emmanuel Viollet-le-Duc begins to publish books about medieval building, renewing interest in castles and showing how they were built.

1869 Work is started on Neuschwanstein, the fairy-tale castle built for King Ludwig II of Bavaria.

Index

Quick-fire Quiz ANSWERS

Page 5 Early Knights
1. a   2. c   3. c   4. b

Page 7 Building a Castle
1. a   2. c   3. b   4. b

Page 9 Castle Designs
1. b   2. a   3. b   4. c

Page 11 Parts of the Castle
1. b   2. b   3. c   4. b

Page 13 Castle Life
1. b   2. a   3. c   4. a

Page 15 Becoming a Knight
1. b   2. b   3. a   4. c

Page 17 Heraldry
1. a   2. c   3. c   4. b

Page 19 Horsemanship
1. a   2. c   3. b   4. b

Page 21 Weapons and Fighting
1. c   2. a   3. a   4. b

Page 23 Armour
1. a   2. b   3. c   4. b

Page 25 Siege
1. b   2. b   3. c   4. b

Page 27 Defence
1. b   2. c   3. a   4. a

Page 29 The Crusades
1. b   2. a   3. c   4. a

Page 31 The Knight's Manor
1. c   2. a   3. c   4. c

Page 33 Peacetime Pursuits
1. c   2. b   3. b   4. a

Page 35 Tournaments
1. c   2. a   3. a   4. b

Page 37 The Last Castles
1. c   2. a   3. b   4. b